Other titles in this series:
Let Your Artist Out!
God's Space in You
Discover Your Spirituality
Give Yourself a Break
Finding The Right Retreat for You
What is Your God like?
Finding Your Centre, a journey with Thomas Merton
Christian Meditation – Your Daily Practice

WHAT DO YOU WANT FROM LIFE?

BRIAN HAWKER

Series editor Jeanne Hinton

For Roger and Keith

Copyright © 1994 Hunt & Thorpe
Text © Brian Hawker
Cover Illustration © Len Munnik

ISBN 1 85608 113 3

In Australia this book is published by:
Hunt & Thorpe Australia Pty Ltd.
9 Euston Street, Rydalmere NSW 2116

All rights reserved. Except for brief quotations in critical articles or reviews, no part of this book may be reproduced in any manner without prior written permission from the publishers. Write to: Hunt & Thorpe, Bowland House, off West Street, Alresford, Hants SO24 9AT

A CIP catalogue record for this book is available from the British Library.

Manufactured in the United Kingdom

CONTENTS

	INTRODUCTION	7
1	DRAWING YOUR LIFE MAP	11
2	FOLLOWING THE FOURFOLD RULE	14
3	GAINING PERSPECTIVE	16
4	CONSIDERING YOUR SPECIAL ABILITIES	21
5	DIGGING THE FOUNDATIONS	28
6	RECOVERING YOUR TRUE SELF	34
7	MAKING A LIFE PLAN	38
8	SHARING YOUR GIFTS	46
9	LETTING GO	52
10	CELEBRATING YOUR JOURNEY	58

■ INTRODUCTION

What do I want from life?

That is a question we will ask over and over again throughout our lives. It is never an easy one; there are so many things to consider. But the complexity of the question is also what makes it such an exciting and absorbing one.

The purpose of this booklet is to help you work at finding an answer at this point in your life journey.

Part of the reason that the question is so complex is that you have to answer it as a member of society. You cannot separate your personal desires and preferences from this larger context, as it will impinge on them anyway.

You may want to be a computer technician, but if there are no openings for you in your area then you have to take that into consideration. It does not mean that you are left with no choice, but that the choice includes moving to another area, which opens up all sorts of other issues.

As we approach the 21st century there are many such issues to consider. Everything is changing so fast that there are few securities left. What was considered normal for our parents or grandparents can no longer be thought of as such. Tradition is no longer the reason that things are done or believed. This means you are forced to think more deeply about what you believe and what is important for you.

While all this means that you have to make up your own mind about what you want for your life, at the same time what you choose has more effect on others than at any other time in history. For you are now part of a global village. Technological advances mean that you can know at the flick of a switch what is happening across the world, and if you are discerning, you will quickly realise just how much what you do affects someone else's life thousands of miles away. An example of this is world trading practices. When you go down to the local store or supermarket, the choices that you make in what you buy may mean the difference between starvation or just enough for another person somewhere else. We are more dependent upon one another than at any other time in history, and this co-dependency can lead either to conflict or co-operation.

At the close of the 20th century we do not know what choices we are going to face in the next few decades. This makes the future even more uncertain. What we do know is that human greed has led to a world that is heavily polluted and has fast depleting resources. In our heart of hearts we know that we must take responsibility. Before you can answer the question: 'What do I want from life?' you need to pause and ask yourself: 'What is my view about life in the 20th century, and what do I want to contribute to its future? What are my views about work, money, the environment and the neighbourhood in which I live? What concerns and interests me about what is happening elsewhere in the world?'

These are important questions, particularly for those who are also wondering: 'What does God want me to do with my life?' Many years ago a man called Micah asked a similar question, answering himself by saying: '... he has told you what he wants, and this is all it is: to be fair and just and merciful, and to walk humbly with your God.' (Micah 6:8)

This is a general direction or attitude, but in this booklet we are dealing with the specific and the concrete – how to draw a map of your life, discover your true Self, identify your gifts, discern the unique purpose of your life and make a life plan.

Let's make a start.

■ 1
DRAWING YOUR LIFE MAP

From the beginning of time God had you and me in mind and also saw the unique contribution each of us could make to the ongoing work of creation. That makes you and me co-creators with God. *Creation is not a static once-and-for-all event; it is ongoing in the purposes of God.* 'God blessed them and said to them, "Be fruitful and increase in number; fill the earth and subdue it. Rule over the fish of the sea and the birds of the air and over every living creature that moves on the ground."' (Genesis 1:28)

God calls each one of us to fulfil our God-given role within the universe. This role or work is uniquely ours; no one else can do it. In discovering it, we discover more about our true Self, the part of us that reflects a part of God's own being. Discovering what we can and were meant to do and putting that discovery into action enables us to become wholly the person we were meant to be, and to be at one with God. The interior peace we will then experience will be the strength that will enable us to go about our work with real conviction. As you seek to find out this purpose, you will have to define your preferences and come to terms with your own personality and desires. God is working with you, not in spite of you! There will be countless questions you will need to ask and answers to be sought within the depth of your being. Be warned. The questions are not easy. Problems abound, but they are the seeds of new opportunities. The journey you are embarking upon requires meditative faith, a lively courage and a strongly disciplined will. However, you are not alone on this journey. God is with you and there are others who are on the same pilgrimage. Together we can deal with the hazards as they arise.

Throughout this book there is a series of short exercises. I encourage you to attempt them as they appear. Try and write a paragraph in answer to each question. There are no right or wrong answers – only an inner awareness of what you are feeling and thinking at the time. Your answers, observations or drawings will make this book personal to you in the process of discovering your life purpose.

■ EXERCISE

1. On a sheet of paper draw a road. On the road mark the various stopping places that have made up the movement of your life from conception to the present moment.

2. Now enlarge your map by drawing in mountains and rivers. The mountains represent the times of struggle when life seemed difficult. The rivers represent the times of peacefulness.

3. Write down your feelings as you look at your life map.

■ 2

FOLLOWING THE FOURFOLD RULE

You have drawn a map of your life using a road to represent movement. Like all movements it will have followed a fourfold rule:

1. Consider that each movement was built upon the foundation of the one before, and that each previous movement had within it some positive goodness, whatever else may have been mixed up in it! It was this goodness that enabled you to grow as a result of those circumstances, and to move on into the next phase of your life. You will have made decisions about which path to take – some of the decisions will have been good and wise, others perhaps not so wise.

Before moving on, acknowledge your own responsibility for each of the actions taken, which will include your reactions to other people's actions. It is important as part of the process you are going through now that you clean the slate. You *made your own decisions*, no matter what or whom may have influenced you. Unless you can acknowledge this, you will project responsibility for your actions onto other people. That will cloud future decisions, and make it difficult for you to see clearly the path that now lies ahead.

2. Movement takes place when we let go of the past in this way, and clear the way for the present moment. Movement is about 'dying to the past'.

3. Progress is made by evaluating what is left after the stage of letting go. This is the time to become acquainted with a newly discovered awareness of your own gifts and how to use them. It is the next step in your journey. This is a new beginning, and it is good.

4. The following step is transforming the new beginning into action which both enables you to grow and enriches others as you go about the work God has entrusted to you.

■ EXERCISE

1. Write a paragraph or draw a picture (you don't have to be a Rembrandt), which expresses your own vision of the future.

2. What do you believe and feel that God requires of you? Have you some vocational calling that you want to fulfil? Write down what it is.

■ 3
GAINING PERSPECTIVE

As you thought about your own life story you may have become aware that there are similarities between some parts of your story and some of the stories told in the bible. Reflecting on this can be a way of helping you gain a better perspective on your own life journey. The bible chronicles the history of God's relationship with his chosen people, and with all humankind. The opening chapters of the bible tell us about the gifts God gave us at creation: light, day, night, sky, earth, sea, vegetation, stars, sun, moon, fish, birds, animals. Each new act of creation is seen and experienced by God as good.

The books of the bible that follow tell of how people both used and abused those gifts. They are also a record of God's persistence in calling people back to his original purpose for them. In story after story in the bible you can discern the fourfold rule we have already looked at. We may be able to recognise part of our story in that of the Exodus, recorded in Exodus 32:31-42, of the people of God moving towards the promised land. Or we may see something of our own experience in the story of the healing of the paralysed man told in Luke 5:18-26, of being healed and enabled to move on. Or again you may have known times of depression and despair when, like Lot's wife, you became bitter about some turn of events (Genesis 19:26), or there may have been times when like Daniel in the furnace you felt you were in a very hot and uncomfortable place (Daniel 3:1-30). Within the bible story it becomes apparent that God was working purposely through the circumstances of the Exodus, the experience of the paralytic, the bitterness of Lot's wife and the burning fire of Daniel. So he is in our lives. It is this purpose that you are now working to discern, or see with more clarity at this particular stage in your life.

This God-given purpose is where the bible story starts. It begins in the Garden of Eden where God puts Adam and Eve in order to 'work it and to tend it'. There is never any suggestion in the bible narrative that the desired Eden will be a place or a time where there is nothing to do. The Hebrew word for 'tend' can also be translated as 'to guard'. Humankind is charged with working or enriching the garden and with guarding its resources. This charge can be perverted into seeking only personal enrichment, and into forgetting God's original intention. Adam and Eve as representative man and woman fell into this trap, and one result was the ensuing pain and toil that then became associated with work. We too will know something of the pain and toil that is associated with work. But we can also know a deep sense of satisfaction that comes from work that is productive and expressive of ourselves as creative persons. Work in the biblical sense involves everything we do: paid work, home work, voluntary work, study work, leisure work, church work – all are creative work in God's purposes. Full-time employment within the modern world suggests an eight-hour paid job for five days of each week. But work in God's purposes is not limited in this way. In this sense we can never be unemployed.

Work that is associated only with pain and toil is a perversion of God's original intention. Work of this kind may be a result of many kinds of injustice, and has been throughout human history, from the slave work undertaken by the Israelites in Egypt to many modern-day equivalents. But the bible story has another thread to it – a turning around or back to God's original intentions. Jesus was involved in this kind of revolution. Throughout his life he demonstrated by his actions alternative ways of perceiving and acting. He looked at the world with the eyes of his Father – the creator of all good gifts. As fully human, Jesus saw and understood the great distress within humankind and by his words and actions he sought to alleviate suffering and to set in motion new ways of being and doing. By the time he began his public ministry, he knew what his purpose was.

'The Spirit of the Lord is on me, because he has anointed me to preach good news to the poor. He has sent me to proclaim freedom for the prisoners and recovery of the sight for the blind, to release the oppressed, to proclaim the year of the Lord's favour.' (Luke 4:18)

At the end his life he knew that he had completed what he had set out to do. Paradoxically, the completion came about in and through suffering.

Whatever we discern the purpose of our life to be, its parameters will change with the cycles of life. The nature of the work you do will change as you move into mid-life and on into life as a senior citizen. Work involves being as much as doing, but the underlying purpose will remain the same. Working out this purpose may involve us in some personal suffering as it did Jesus. This presents us with a choice – to continue onwards, or to turn back.

■ EXERCISE

1. How do you understand the word work?

2. What has been your experience of work to date?

3. What bible stories come to mind that bear a resemblance to some of your life experiences? Take one or two stories and read them again. What do they tell you about your own experiences, and about your responses to God's call on your life?

■ 4
CONSIDERING YOUR SPECIAL ABILITIES

YOUR SPECIAL ABILITIES or gifts are the basic materials that enable you to live purposefully and to make a life plan.

'Now God gives us many kinds of special abilities, but it is the same Spirit who is the source of them all,' it says in one of the books of the New Testament (1 Corinthians 12:4).

Gifts come in many different packages and from various sources. In some cases the wrapping is lavish, promising good things to come, and in others the gift may not seem to be worth the wrapping! Others are less well presented, and yet turn out to be priceless. Some gifts we welcome, others we dislike. Some gifts pose problems – we are not sure what they are or how to use them.

Gifts are (or should be) given voluntarily and freely. There are no price tags attached. We are free to do whatever we like with them, even to the point of giving them away.

Gifts from God are given with a purpose. They are given to be understood and used. The nature of God as giver is such that the gifts will never be out of date. They hold within themselves the potential to be used in many different ways throughout life. The gifts of natural ability are not to be squandered or thrown away. Not, that is, if we want to find satisfaction.

The preacher whose words are recorded for us in the book of Ecclesiastes in the Old Testament tells us, 'that everyone may eat and drink, and find satisfaction in all his toil – this is the gift of God.' What gifts have you been given?

■ EXERCISE

Make a list of all gifts or special abilities you are aware of – those that make you *you*.

As you make this list, become aware of those gifts that have been passed on to you through others – what you learnt from parents or grandparents or other significant adults in your life, subjects you were taught at school or university and taught in a way that helped you discover your interests and skills.

Record people who have been gifts to you, those who helped you on your way – family members, teachers, doctors, friends. God's gifts to us come through such human sources, and it is in relationship to these others that we discover ourselves. In thinking about this exercise in this way you may find you recall interests and abilities you had long since forgotten or buried. Now may be the time to remember!

Don't forget while making your list to write down the natural but essential gifts of sight, hearing, smell, taste and touch. You may lack one of these abilities, but if so it is likely that you have compensated for this by developing another or others more highly. Whether this is so or not, one or more of these natural abilities may already be highly developed in you. This is a gift. There are other gifts we have received. The ability to be sensitive to others, to be compassionate, to encourage others, or to make them laugh. Let your list be as broad as you can make it.

Special gifts suggest a giver who knows you, your likes and dislikes, your needs and desires.

When you unpack a gift that excites you, you will want to put it to use. It has been given for this purpose, not to be hoarded or put aside and forgotten. Unless we use our gifts, our special abilities, they will begin to lose something of their 'giftedness'. If you have put down 'to make someone laugh' as one of your abilities, then you need to use this ability, or you will lose it. God as giver gives lavishly and appropriately, but he also gives gifts for a purpose – to be used. They enable us to function as co-creators with God, to make our own contribution to the world which is continually being created.

■ EXERCISE

1. Look again at your list of gifts.

2. How have you used the gifts you have been given? Here is an example. One person wrote down that he had a gift for languages, and spoke German fluently. At an early stage he chose to use that gift by becoming a teacher. Later in retirement he used the same gift to help businessmen and women develop their understanding and use of the language. Later still he was considering using the gift to discover more about German literature, and had in mind offering to facilitate a small group exploration of the subject. The use of our gifts can differ at various times of our lives, and indeed this is a good thing, as we are growing ourselves in the process.

3. How many gifts have you stored away, thinking they may become handy later in life? Another person listed that she had been good at drawing at school, but had never developed this skill beyond her school years. She had always thought that at some point in the future she would take the time to do so. Faced in mid-life with early retirement, she decided to take day classes in art and later went on to complete a university degree. She is now illustrating books!

Look at each one of the gifts you have listed, and ask yourself some questions. In what ways have I used that ability? In what other ways could I explore its use? Is it a gift I want to develop more fully now? Other questions will come to mind as you do this. There may even be subjects you did not do well in at school that you now find you want to explore. As some teachers

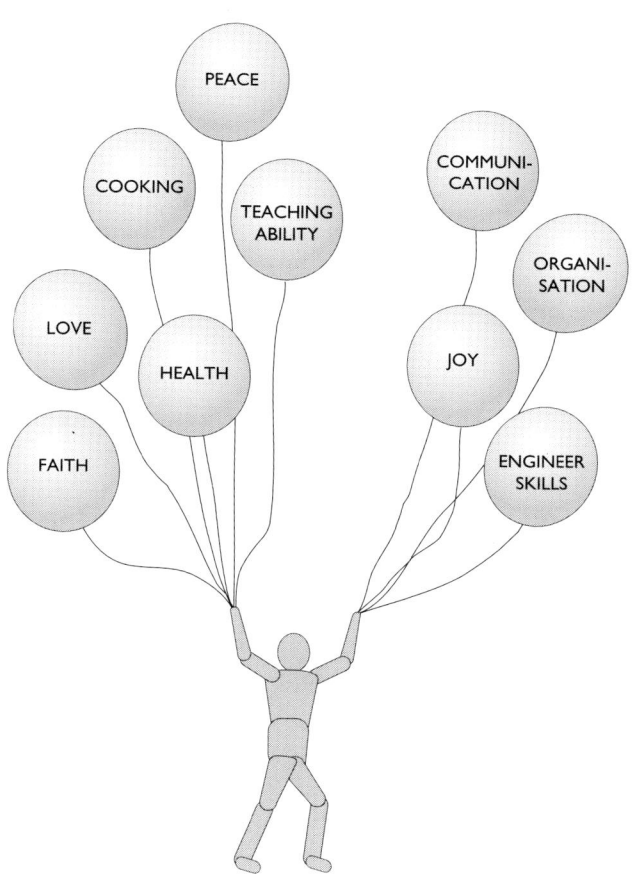

can help us develop in particular subjects, others may have the opposite effect! If there is an ability or interest you have felt cheated out of, stop and think why you feel this way – it may be an indication that you do have an ability in this area. You may want to list this too – with a question mark or symbol to express what you feel about it.

4. Draw a stick picture of yourself and surround it with coloured balloons, each one bearing the name of a different gift you have been given. Celebrate yourself. This is important, and what God intended. He wants us to enjoy ourselves; this is a part of what the gift of joy is about.

5. Balloons suggest a party. Why not throw a party, using some of your gifts. To go back to my example of the person who listed German as one of his accomplishments, he decided to have a German party with German food, dances, music, and stories. Another person who had listed the ability to love as an attribute, decided to celebrate the gift of love, and chose to do this one Valentine's Day!

Life is good, celebrate it!

■ 5
DIGGING THE FOUNDATIONS

LIFE IS A SERIES of stages which build one upon another. During each stage we learn various skills, which help us to pass on to the next. Each stage forms a journey. This is a movement, an exciting adventure to enjoy.

During the first journey we dig the foundations. This is the ego-building stage, trying to understand how *I* can become *me*. There are many ways in which this search expresses itself: 'I'm going to be a bus driver when I grow up', or, 'I want to be a nurse'.

'What am I going to be?' is an important question. Finding the answer can take us into our mid-20s or beyond, and even then we may only be beginning to find an answer. We are all born with an inner core or essence which is called the Self. *It is this Self which is made in the image of God.* It is the *I am-ness* of your unique being. This inner core is very vulnerable and has a world outside of itself to deal with, which appears very threatening. For the first nine months of your life your connection with this world is experienced through the care or otherwise of parents or parental figures. You have no experience of yourself apart from them. But gradually your are weaned from that dependence, and experience yourself as an individual apart from them, responding to the outside world on your own terms.

In this first vulnerable stage we all seek to protect our fragile inner core by putting something like a barbed wire fence around this Self. This defence mechanism requires that you build another, not really true self, from which to operate in relation to the outside world. This 'false self' is what is called the ego – a persona or chosen role.

How you develop this role will depend a lot on outward circumstances, and on those who bring you up. A perfectionist parent will require you to do everything right. Your reaction may be to be constantly on your guard to ensure that nothing you do displeases others, particularly those in authority. You could be the child of over-protective parents, and may respond by becoming very needy, in order to continue to gain attention. Or your parents may be so busy attending to their own lives and work that you are never sure who you are at all. The outcome may be that you are constantly changing your own responses in order to fit into whatever is happening around you, trying to be all things to all people.

If you come from temperamental stock, then you may well have to defend yourself against histrionic outbursts or long melancholic stories of what might have been. Again, if you are made to tiptoe past the study because mother or father is busy, you could well react by withdrawing into your own ego world. Your response then to many circumstances in life will be to withdraw rather than to confront.

In all of these responses, your ego personality is being formed, and the persona or role is also then the person you present to others.

The messages that you receive from others are

also part of an inner reaction that can decide how you are going to spend your life. 'Get a good education and you'll be alright,' is the dictum of many parents, but you may get a different message from your peers – that you are a prig, not interested in making friends. You then have a difficult decision to make – whether to please your parents by studying hard and being top of the class, or going out with your friends and hoping to get by in the examinations. To get the balance right demands a compromise and a difficult decision may have to be made. An immature person tries to please everyone, afraid to be decisive in case it leads to a rejection either by parents on whom they have come to rely or by their peers from whom they want acceptance.

Messages come to us in all sorts of different ways on our first journey. You may well have been told, 'It is better to wear out than to rust out,' and have become a workaholic, or 'Look after the pennies and the pounds will look after themselves', and become a bit of a miser. Such proverbs have a profound effect on us as we grow up. Other communications deal with judgments made about people or particular nationalities or religions.

How you react to all of these stimuli forms your personality, your character and all that others call *you*. Much, but not all of this, is false. The true Self remains hidden within, and from time to time you may feel uncomfortably aware that you are acting rather than being who you really are.

In this first journey you are seeking to develop an acceptable persona that allows you to live without too much hassle. As a consequence you may well take on your parents' expectations without thinking them through. You are becoming the doctor or the accountant they expect or want you to be. You may see the world and others through their eyes, not your own, and take on their political persuasion without deciding what you think for yourself.

All this is about digging the foundations. It is during this phase that you developed many of the gifts you have already listed. If you look at the list again now, you may be aware that some of what you have written is not really you at all, but your response to others' expectations.

At some point in this ego-building first journey there comes a crisis point. It may be a religious conversion (if this happens early in life then a second conversion may well be necessary). It may be the death or divorce of parents, the collapse of a business or a change of schools. Later it could be circumstances that surround your chosen job which suddenly lead to an understanding of the unfulfilled potential of the true Self. You become aware that much of your life seems a sham and that you need to look at other ways of expressing yourself.

This crisis point forms the launching pad for the second journey.

■ EXERCISE

1. What parental messages are you aware of that you still feel you must obey?

2. Can you recall a crisis point that led you to a deeper understanding of yourself? Are you at such a crisis point now? If so, what has led to this present crisis?

■ 6
RECOVERING YOUR TRUE SELF

THE SECOND JOURNEY is coming home to your true Self. In this journey you are building yourself a home in which you feel comfortable with yourself. This involves an understanding of our interior growth. This journey of the recovery of your true Self is what Carl Jung, the Swiss psychologist, called the path of individuation.

The first journey was necessary to this second one. During this initial journey, you needed your defences in order to learn how to respond to the outer world. During this phase you will have dug the foundations for the house or home that is you, and acquired some bricks for its building. The bricks are the gifts you have already listed as yours. As the first and second floors of this building grow, so you will be enabled to deepen your relationships with others and with God. It is a home to be shared.

Outwardly the second journey may look very similar to the first, but this journey is different in that only you can take it. It will not be at the prompting of others, but of an inner prompting or urging that gives the strength and motivation to pursue it. This inner prompting comes from God, who knows us better than we know ourselves.

At the start of this journey it is helpful to reflect on your relationship with God up to this point. What has been your experience of God? You may have had a conversion experience at an early age, and made a commitment then to Jesus as Saviour. Or, there may have come a crisis point when a difficult situation caused you to turn to God. The number of people who make a commitment to Christ when in prison, in the throes of divorce or when told of an incurable disease is quite staggering. Whether through a sudden conversion or a more gradual awakening, it is your relationship with God that will enable you to make the leap of faith that will take you from a first journey into a second.

Knowing that we are safe in God's hands, we can allow our ego-self to diminish, our masks to drop. This enables us now to react not to parental directions or to our own expectations of prestige, power or material security, but to the guidance of the Holy Spirit.

What is the real purpose of your life? This is the vital question in this second journey. God is the architect and the builder. It is in surrendering the ego-self to God that we discover the real life that Jesus offers, and become in tune with God's purpose rather than continuing our own egocentric striving. We will never be able to live wholly ego-free during this life, but we can move a long way in this direction.

Now is the time to move on to make a life plan, or to what is often called a discernment process. This bring us back again to those bricks – the gifts you listed earlier. The list contains all you need for the making of this plan. Now in the second journey these gifts will be internalised to give meaning to being rather than *doing*. What you do begins to flow easily and comfortably from who you know yourself to be.

■ EXERCISE

1. Review the list of your gifts.

2. What is God's purpose for you? Look again at your earlier answer to the question of vocational calling. Does that adequately express what you feel about God's purpose for you, or do you want to change or add to it? At this stage make the statement about purpose as broad as possible. For example, 'To show others that the gifts I have received can be used for myself and others.'

■ 7
MAKING A LIFE PLAN

IN THE MAKING of your life plan you become more specific about what you have already written. First, take some time considering the possibilities that follow from what you have already stated. For example, 'My interest in, and the gifts I have received point to work in the Third World, utilising alternative technology.' Or, 'As a mother, to ensure that my children receive every care and attention, and that we as a family are aware of the gifts we have been given and are enabled to share them.'

Now, at this early stage, it is likely that you may need to consult with others. A life plan has to be looked at from four viewpoints, for example:

1. An interest in alternative technologies
2. Appropriate engineering skills
3. Your own feelings about future direction and
4. Its effect upon others.

You will not be popular if your final stated

purpose has not taken your spouse, family or other committed relationships into account. Having stated your purpose a conference with others could be the next step. Together work on an agreed statement about purpose, you may then have something like this, 'Together with my partner, to work towards ...'

Once you have got this far, *stop*. With your piece of paper in front of you and your purpose written down, offer the whole of your life anew to God. Now is the time for the discernment process.

First, listen to the reasons why you consider what you have written to be the right way forward. List them.

On the next day or during the next week, listen to the reasons *against* such a decision. Write these down.

During the following day or week, ask yourself about the unknowns in the proposed way forward. What more do I need to know about this project, and how can I find out the answers to the questions? When you have found the answers to these questions, put the matter aside for a month.

At the end of the month, come back to your discernment paper, re-read it and, in prayer, make your decision. 'Yes, this is the way forward,' or 'No, this not the way forward.'

If you are at peace and those around you in agreement with the decision, then you are ready to proceed with the next step. If not, take a breather and then start the whole process over again. This is important work!

■ LOOK AHEAD

Having decided what your life purpose is, you are now ready to take the next step and look ahead at the next ten years.

In a period of quiet prayer, ask God to show you how your life will be in ten years time. On a sheet of paper list the things that you consider will be different in your life. You may have married, had children and written your first novel. Perhaps you will have moved from your present situation, emigrated, learnt a new language or other skill. Whatever the conjectures, record them.

■ LIST THE TASKS

Once that list is as complete as you can make it, write another which includes all the tasks that will have to be done in order to bring about the ten-year goal. Take the idea of learning a new language as an example:

1. I will have to find out where I can learn Japanese.

2. Can I find
   (a) a private tutor
   (b) an evening class
   (c) a correspondence course?

3. When am I going go to find this out?

4. How do I feel about it?

Make this sort of list for all the tasks to be dealt with during the ten-year period. Try to record your feelings about them as well. You may suddenly realise that you will have to leave your parental family and possibly never see them again. How do you feel about that? Such a possibility involves a dying, and we will be looking at this aspect when we come to the fourth and final journey. If the vision of the future is the right one then the difficulties and sadness involved have to be faced along with the joy of life's movement.

■ FIVE YEARS AHEAD

If you still feel inwardly at peace about the way ahead, do the same exercise but this time for the next five year period of your life.

■ NEXT STEPS

Now your decision is going to be made more concrete still. Do the exercise for the third time, but this time concentrate on what has to be done during the coming year. You may have to give up your present job, die to your singleness, move house, buy a car. There may be financial pressures resulting from these decisions.

At this stage, reflect quietly again on what you are proposing. How do your friends feel about it? How do you feel now? Are you scared, or prepared to go through with it. Or, even, does the whole project now feel wrong? If the latter, begin again.

To begin again will seem daunting after all this effort. Give yourself time and space. In meditative prayer, ask again, 'What *is* it I am called to do and be?' The answer may be to continue working at the tasks that are already yours, but to develop new skills or outlets. If so, complete the ten, five-year and next steps exercises around this answer.

■ TODAY

Now comes the really difficult bit!

What has to be done *today* in order to make the plan work? What is the first step? It might be that you have decided to write to a language school, or find out how to get to India. It could be that you need to make radical proposals within your present area of work. Whatever it is, make sure that it is completed today.

I have found that having stated my goals and the way I expect to attain them, there is a need within me to do something towards them each day. If I find myself complaining that I have been very busy all day but seem to have accomplished very little, then I look again at the goal towards which I feel God is calling me. Usually in such a situation I realise that I may have done a lot during the day but nothing that has drawn me closer to my goal. To be able to tick off, as completed, a particular task towards the goal acts as a stimulus, encouraging me to go on.

For some, this process of looking ahead and listing tasks may feel too constricting. Life for them has always seemed to flow in the right direction and things have been completed in the end. This relaxed attitude to the way ahead is OK but the tasks may well take longer to complete. Do remember we don't have unlimited time to complete our life purpose!

A further warning – don't kill yourself trying to get everything done in the first year. You have looked ahead ten years, then five years and then one year. Plan the time, always giving yourself 50 per cent more than you judge the project will take. If you have to write a letter that should take ten minutes to complete, allow fifteen minutes for the task. You might complete the letter in ten minutes, but if the 'phone rings or someone comes to the door it could take a lot longer, and you have cushioned yourself against that eventuality. If you think you are going to learn Japanese in a year, then allow eighteen months. You might not need the extra months but they are there in case you do, and you are not threatened by a shortage of time.

In working out the plan remember that you are interdependent. This means that your relationships with others are very important and need to be maintained not only for your own sake, but for the sake of all our futures. If this does not happen then the whole process will have been a failure, because it will have remained an ego-centred first journey exercise rather than a genuine call towards your co-creative role in God's world. Which brings us back to the journeys, and to the third journey that is there for us to make.

■ 8
SHARING YOUR GIFTS

THE THIRD JOURNEY, which is sometimes called the wisdom journey, flows naturally from the other two. It has to do with a different orientation of ourselves and our gifts – a different kind of lifestyle.

I can perhaps explain what I mean best by using Jesus himself as an example. Jesus made the same kind of journeys that we are all called to make. Like us there was a time when he had to find out about himself in the first journey of life. He came to this point early on. By the age of twelve Jesus knew who he was and that he had a purpose in life. He made this clear when he explained to his worried parents that he had 'to be in his Father's house, (Luke 2:41-52). However, to fulfil his Father's purpose he still had to mature to full manhood. His trade as a carpenter and his place in his family and village, helped him in this process.

There came the time, however, when an inner

prompting pushed him further on his journey. There were bigger and deeper issues to face at this point. His baptism by John gave him a further confirmation of his relationship to the Father. He heard a voice from heaven proclaiming, 'You are my son, whom I love; with you I am well pleased.' In the wilderness, following this experience, Jesus faced the identity question at an even deeper level. What kind of son? What kind of person? For Jesus the questions, as for us, centred around the ideas and expectations of others. Should he be a social wonder worker, turning stones into bread, or a political dictator ruling the world, or some kind of magician performing spectacular feats of personal bravery? Read about it in Luke 4:1-12.

Jesus rejected all these possibilities and came up with his own stated goal. It was 'to preach good news to the poor, recovery of sight to the blind, and to release the oppressed.' For his courage in stating this purpose he was rejected by the people with whom he had grown up. They took him to the brow of a hill in order to throw him down and kill him. Hardly a encouraging start to this part of his journey! Jesus had to make his own way, without their support.

The kind of life discernment that comes from a second journey has to be lived out in the nitty gritty of life. This is what makes it such a difficult journey to live. Jesus' third journey was outwardly expressed in his teaching, in healing the sick and in the miraculous signs that accompanied his proclamation of the kingdom of God. But the life that those who witnessed these events experienced flowed not from the outward events themselves but from a deeper reality, from Jesus' own inner life and being.

The wisdom expressed in the third journey is that which enables us to keep growing and maturing in this inner place. Jesus learnt how to do this, and many times withdrew from the company of others in order to maintain this inner sense of who he was and what he was about. He knew it was important that his ministry was not carried out for his own aggrandisement. That would have been to give in to the temptations he had faced in the desert. Jesus had to make sure that it was the Father who was glorified in all these events, that people experienced the very nature of the Father through and in the events, and in their encounters with himself. Jesus revealed the true nature of his Father by confronting those who opposed him with love not with hatred, by honouring life and those who suffered because of their oppression and marginalisation by others.

For us, too, living this third journey will mean coming to a new understanding of our interdependence, of how to seek co-operation rather than competition, and of how our gifts can be used not only for our benefit but for the benefit of the whole community.

As we live at this deeper level we will experience a change in the way we live our lives. Increasingly, a stillness and sureness of direction will fill our activities. Our prayer life will begin to have as its focus the desire to be united wholly with God in working out his purposes. We will find that inwardly we desire more and more that our gifts are shared with others, and that they might enable others to share their gifts. We will be concerned that God's kingdom of justice and

Diagram: Life Purpose Wheel

PURPOSE (centre): Together with my family to enjoy a healthy body and soul and to use my gifts and skills as an engineer for the community

Main segments and sub-segments:

- **HOME WORK**: Garden; House Maintenance; Family
- **PAID WORK**: Engineer; Consultant to Xtn Aid; Consultant Inter Aid
- **VOLUNTARY WORK**: Car Maintain. with Youth Club; Samaritans
- **CHURCH WORK**: Services; House Group; Prayer Group; Bible Study; Choir
- **LEISURE WORK**: Keep Fit; Badminton; Swimming; Theatre
- **STUDY WORK**: Japanese Course; Writing Engineering Projects

---

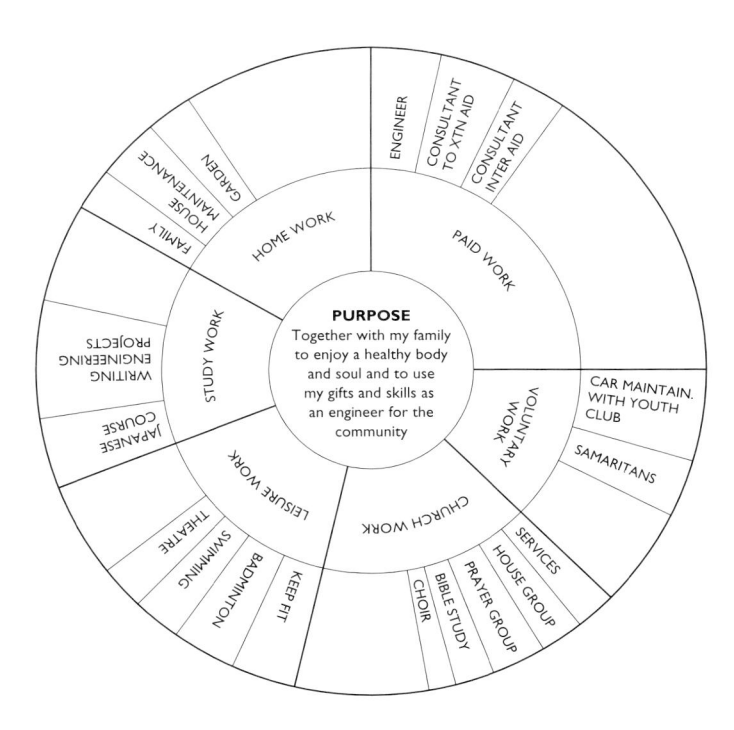

peace becomes a tangible reality in the areas of life in which we move.

As we develop with this new orientation, we will realise that the divisions between paid employment and the other kinds of work that we engage in are no longer there. All flow from one peaceful centre, our inner sense of Self.

The following exercise is a useful tool for maintaining this kind of balance in your life.

■ EXERCISE

1. Draw three concentric circles (rather like a target). In the inner circle write down your purpose. Dissect the second circle into as many segments as are necessary. Name each segment with the way you spend your time (ie paid work, home work, voluntary work, church work, leisure work etc). In the outer circle, extend the segments and write down each thing you do that makes up the inner segment (ie voluntary work in the second circle could be extended in the third circle to work at the children's home, work with the youth club etc).

2. Ask yourself, do circles two and three help you to carry out your purpose? If not, then what has to be allowed to die in order that your purpose can be achieved?

■ 9
LETTING GO

THIS BRINGS US to the an understanding of the fourth and final journey.

Jesus in his own personal journey knew what it was not only to honour life, but also to understand the necessity of death. Inwardly, he had confronted the passage through death, long before he was taken and suffered the painful death of crucifixion. This too he saw to be part of the journey he was called upon to undertake. The fourth journey was expressed both in his passion and death, and in the various ways in which, throughout his life, he underwent a series of little deaths.

Jesus experienced a dying in the temple when he was only twelve years old. He had to die to the security of his dependence on his earthly parents, Joseph and Mary, in order to serve in his Father's house. To make this passage he stayed behind in Jerusalem when the others were on their way home. Precipitously, like all adolescents, he wanted to start on the new experience immediately. In being willing to continue to live in his parents' home, to be obedient to them and to learn a trade as a craftsman, he experienced another kind of death, necessary to his maturing into adulthood.

Later, when it was time for him to take up his own life work, he underwent another little death when he was rejected by those who knew him best. He had to die to the familiar town in which he had grown up, in order to take on the ministry mapped out for him by his awareness of the divine purpose.

Another little death happened later when he realised and was able to express in words that his mother and brothers were not only those given to him physically but all those who did the will of his Father. It cost him and his blood family some pain to speak about this openly (Luke 8:19-21).

Death confronts us all in these many lesser ways throughout our lifetime, and long before we face the inevitability of our actual physical death. In our culture, death is rarely mentioned in conversation or faced in our thoughts, yet continual dying is a necessary part of all four journeys.

In the first journey which deals with our human development through childhood to adolescence and adulthood, we have to come to terms with each of the various stages we pass through if the next phase is to have any real hope of being attained. Later, there are many such passages to navigate. In order to enter the married state you must allow the single state to die. If you get married and nothing dies inwardly of your single stage, then the new married life will never be fully lived. The result will be unhappiness for all involved. If you change your job but continually return to the scene of your former employment, then you are not allowing the new job to take its rightful place in your life. As a parent, if you continue to think of your adult children as little girls or boys, then you are refusing to allow that period of their lives to die, and you block, in your own mind, their attainment of full adulthood. At the same time, you refuse to allow this stage in your own life to die, blocking your own next stage of development.

The fourth journey also brings us into the realm of physical death. With the advances of medical practice, transplant surgery and the lengthening of our life span there seems to be an unspoken assumption that death is to be feared and avoided for as long as possible. Physical death is seen as a tragedy. Of course it often is for those who are left behind, but not for the one who is dying. If faith in our personal surrender to God's control is authentic then we have nothing to fear in letting go of human life. This is the ultimate letting go in order that the true life we seek may be lived out fully in the presence of God.

There is an in-built grief process that is a part of living this fourth journey, which has to be faced again and again throughout your lifetime. Understanding what is involved in this grieving process is important. When someone dies, you are shocked. You will find it hard at first to believe that the death has taken place. As a result you may become withdrawn or depressed. You are likely to feel and need to express your anger – with God, with the person who has died and with yourself for not having done enough. In the process of time you then move towards a point of accepting what has happened, and are then able to get on with your own life, adapting to the new situation. The same process takes place in other circumstances too. You need to be able to grieve over the loss of your single status when you get married; to do the same when you move house, take up a new job, or move into any new situation in life. If you do not give yourself the time or permission to grieve over what has been lost or to express your feelings of distress at what has taken place, then you will not reach the place of acceptance that enables you to live fully the next stage. Continual dying is about allowing the last moment to go so that the next may really be.

It is as this fourth stage of the journey is completed that the house that is you is completed. I liken it to the roof being put on the house, so that the scaffolding can at last come down. It is difficult to imagine what a house would feel when suddenly exposed to the world for the first time! But you cannot live in the scaffolding of life for ever. Each of us in realising our potential reflects God's image in us, an image not to be hidden, but fully and openly shared with all others. That comes from a new spontaneity of life and expression – a new freedom to be and to do.

■ EXERCISE

1. What has been your experience of loss? Have you grieved your losses?

2. What areas of your life have to be allowed to die in order that you can become fully the person God has called you to be?

3. What do you feel about physical death?

■ 10
CELEBRATING YOUR JOURNEY

The story of creation told in Genesis, in the opening chapters of the bible, tells how God created the world in an ordered way. For each day there was a task that God completed. Then there was a pause as the work of each day was evaluated: 'and God looked, and it was very good.' This awareness of the divine goodness inherent in the creative process is an important part of the process itself. This recognition of inner goodness means we take time to reflect, give thanks and celebrate. The spaces, represented by the days, in the Genesis account of creation are important. There is evening, followed again by the light of morning. In any new creative plan there is often a feeling of darkness that follows the first creative inspiration. This darkness may well be experienced as interior and depressive. Such darkness may include a sense of uncertainty about the decisions made, a feeling of unworthiness that one might not be able to accomplish the proposed project; a sense of grief as one contemplates the loss and letting go that arises from the new direction. All of these feelings of vulnerability are no bad thing. We can encourage ourselves by remembering that God looks upon our humanity – upon you and me – as basically good, made in the Divine image. By appropriating for ourselves this gift of goodness we can gain the courage and faith to move on. Darkness is overcome by light, if we are not afraid of the dark in the first place.

By celebrating life – its many journeys – we keep alive the movement inherent in these journeys. Not everyone completes all the four journeys. Some will stay with the first ego-building journey throughout their lives. Others will pass on to the second journey and become immersed in its questions, but never fully risk moving on to test the answers. Others still will live their third journey of wisdom with confidence. All of us will know the fourth journey of continual dying. Once we have absorbed the information necessary for each phase of the journey we pass on to the next vital growth point, but no one wholly completes any of the journeys, for there is always more to learn, absorb and put into practice. Once the basics of the first journey have become a part of the self, then the possibilities of moving on to the delights and despairs of the other journeys are open to those who choose that path.

Marking the movements that are a part of these journeys helps to keep us moving. There is no need to wait for a retirement party to celebrate our life's journeys! Celebrate beginnings, middles and endings! It may be in the form of a special meal or trip to the theatre or concert hall. Whatever it is, be sure and do it!

■ EXERCISE

1. Can you see the pattern of the four journeys within your own life experience?

2. In what ways have you celebrated your life passages? What form of celebration do you like most?

3. Are you at ease celebrating *you*? What part and form could celebration take as you continue with your journey?

■ A POSTSCRIPT

When you have completed the first year towards your goal, re-read this book and your answers to the exercises, then update the whole plan.